D0571140

—◆—

"My aim is to express in a natural way what I feel, what is in me, both rhythmically and spiritually."

—William H. Johnson

DIEGO RIVERA. *The Flower Vendor (Girl with Lilies).*
1941. Oil on Masonite, 48 × 48″. Norton Simon Museum, Pasadena, CA, Gift of Mr. Cary Grant, 1980. © 2007 Banco de México
Diego Rivera & Frida Kahlo Museums Trust. Av. Cinco de Mayo No. 2, Col. Centro, Del. Cuauhtémoc 06059, México, D.F.

COME
LOOK WITH ME

Exploring Modern Art

Jessica Noelani Wright

BANK STREET COLLEGE OF EDUCATION

Charlesbridge

Copyright © assigned 2006 to Charlesbridge Publishing

While every effort has been made to obtain permission from the artists and copyright holders of the works herein, there may be cases where we have been unable to contact a copyright holder. The publisher will be happy to correct any omission in future printings.

All rights reserved, including the right of reproduction in whole or in part in any form. Charlesbridge and colophon are registered trademarks of Charlesbridge Publishing, Inc.

Published by Charlesbridge
85 Main Street
Watertown, MA 02472
(617) 926-0329
www.charlesbridge.com

Originally published by Lickle Publishing, Inc.

Library of Congress Control Number
2002103900

ISBN-13: 978-1-890674-10-6 (reinforced for library use)
ISBN-10: 1-890674-10-9 (reinforced for library use)

Series producer: Charles Davey
Edited by Bank Street College of Education,
Andrea Perelman, Project Manager

Production & Design: Charles Davey *design* LLC
Printed and bound by C & C Offset Printing Co. Ltd.
in Shenzhen, Guangdong, China

(hc) 19 18 17 16

Contents

Preface

What makes a cow look like a cow? Is it the animal's color? Its shape? How can it look different from an ordinary cow, yet still clearly be a cow? Many modern artists asked questions such as these that challenge conventional assumptions about art. In response, these artists exaggerated, distorted, and fictionalized their imagery. In short, they used their imagination to express their own very personal visions.

In this study of Western modern art from the late nineteenth and early twentieth centuries, the attempt is not to create a comprehensive survey of art. Instead, *Come Look with Me: Exploring Modern Art* will introduce children to the choices artists make when they transform what they see into something new. Through the questions presented in the book, children are encouraged to describe what they see, analyze how the artist has put elements together in deliberate compositions, and develop informed opinions about a work of art. No previous knowledge of art history is required. These studies of artworks—which include an all-red dining room, a magnified leaf, and even a yellow cow—will encourage children to appreciate the directions that the human imagination can take.

How to use this book

COME LOOK WITH ME: *Exploring Modern Art* is part of a series of interactive art appreciation books for children. Like the other books in the series, this one can be shared with one child or a small group of children. Each of the twelve works of art is paired with a set of questions meant to stimulate thoughtful discussion between adults and children. The accompanying text, which gives background information on the artist and the work, can be read silently or aloud by the adult while the children look at the illustrations.

Ask a child to point to part of the image while he or she discusses it. When working with a group, ask if anyone has a different idea. There are no right or wrong answers to the questions, and everyone will benefit from the different perspectives that experience, age, and personal taste can bring to a group discussion. To keep the interaction lively, it is best to limit each session to the discussion of two or three works of art.

This book can be used in the classroom, at home, and of course, in museums. There is no substitute for a visit to a museum to see the color and texture of an artist's brush strokes and to take in the size of an original artwork. However, the methods given here can help children learn a way of looking at original works of art and encourage them to share their understanding with others.

HENRI MATISSE. *The Red Room (Harmony in Red)*.
1908. Oil on canvas, 71¹⁄₁₆ × 87″. Hermitage Museum, St. Petersburg, Russia. © 2008 Succession H. Matisse /
Artists Rights Society (ARS), New York. Photograph © Bridgeman Art Library, London / SuperStock.

Where do you see straight lines in this painting? Where do you see curved lines? Do there seem to be more straight lines or curved ones?

Why do you think Matisse chose to paint the room red instead of blue or green?

What do you think the woman in the painting is doing? How do you think she feels?

What kinds of feelings would you get from being in this room?

Although Henri Matisse (1869 –1954) failed in his first attempt at the entrance examination to France's best art school, he continued with his art. Today he is renowned as one of the finest artists who ever lived. While he is most famous for his paintings, Matisse produced other kinds of art too: sculpture, prints, and artworks known as collages. He made these collages using sheets of paper in various colors. He cut different shapes out of the sheets and pasted them onto a flat surface to create a picture.

Matisse believed a painter should rely on his instinct and allow the colors and shapes in a painting to show the artist where they should be positioned. For this reason, he often painted expressive forms first and added details later. He was considered the leader of a group of painters called the "fauves," French for "wild beasts." Critics gave them this name because of the "wild" bright colors and distorted shapes they used in their paintings.

The bright colors, flat shapes, and curving lines in *The Red Room (Harmony in Red)* make it a typical example of Matisse's work from this period. During this time, he painted pictures with dramatically simplified areas of pure color and strong patterns, in which figures and objects appear to be flat. However, in this picture, Matisse has added an illusion of three-dimensional depth by giving us a window that shows the world outside the red room.

Buffalo Mask,
(Baulé, Ivory Coast).
Wood, 28" high.
Musée d'Art moderne de Troyes,
Gift of Pierre and Denise Lévy.

PABLO PICASSO. *Horse Head Mask,* from Massine's ballet "Parade."
Painted wood and hemp. Reconstruction and realization supervised by
Kermit Love for the Joffrey Ballet's 1974 production. © 2008 Estate of Pablo
Picasso / Artists Rights Society (ARS), New York. Photo © Migdoll 2002.

What shapes can you find in each of these masks?

In what ways are the two masks alike? In what ways are they different?

What materials do you think were used to make each of the masks?

If you were to put on one of the masks, which one would you choose? What kind of character would you become?

Nearly everyone has heard of Picasso! Born in Spain, Pablo Ruiz y Picasso (1881–1973) was one of the most famous artists who ever lived. He is particularly famous for his changing styles over the years. Picasso constantly sought new ways to express himself and was always receptive to the influences of art from other cultures.

African art was one such influence. In the early 1900s, many European artists became fascinated by the designs of objects such as masks, fabrics, furniture, and sculpture then being imported from Africa. Picasso found African masks especially interesting and began to create his own, incorporating elements of African styles.

This African mask is one type Picasso might have seen. A "firespitter" mask from the Ivory Coast in Africa, it was worn at night in a ritual dance meant to scare away negative spiritual and natural forces that might harm the crops and herds of a farming community. The patterns of these masks were a combination of several different ferocious animals in order to make them as scary as possible.

Picasso's mask shown here is a copy of his original, which was made for a ballet performance. Its design shows how Picasso was influenced by African art's shapes and styles, as well as its purpose. Both of these masks were worn by a dancer. Picasso's mask was worn by a dancer in a ballet, the African mask by a dancer warning away negative forces.

FRANZ MARC. *Yellow Cow (Gelbe Kuh)*.
1911. Oil on canvas, 55⅜ × 74½". Solomon R. Guggenheim Museum, New York.
Solomon R. Guggenheim Founding Collection. 49.1210.

Describe the animal you see in this painting. Describe the background scene.

Does this scene look like one you might see in real life? In what ways has the artist used his imagination in painting this scene?

Does this look like a calm, quiet scene or an active, loud one? What makes you think so?

As a young man, Franz Marc (1880–1916) participated in the strong back-to-nature movement then developing in his native Germany. Believing that close contact with the land would revitalize them, many people were drawn to artists' groups in rural areas. Marc was especially interested in animals because he regarded them as magnificent spiritual creatures. He finally decided to create paintings only of animals in their natural surroundings.

Marc and a fellow painter, Vasily Kandinsky, shared some of the same ideas. They formed an artists' group called *Der Blaue Reiter*, which means "The Blue Rider" in German (the name came from the title of a painting by Kandinsky). The group became recognized for its pioneering of abstraction, a method in which the artist adds or omits elements in order to produce a simple design. Marc and his colleagues sought to express certain feelings and ideas by using very bright, non-naturalistic colors to make their paintings look different from real life. They hoped that as a result viewers would experience strong emotional and spiritual responses to their pictures.

In *Yellow Cow*, we can see how Marc used animals and bright colors in his art. For Marc, the color yellow always symbolized a female, the color blue symbolized a male. Some art historians believe Marc might have painted this picture to celebrate his marriage. If this is so, then the frolicking yellow cow is Marc's bride, and Marc himself is the blue mountain in the background.

JOHN SLOAN. *Backyards, Greenwich Village.*
1914. Oil on canvas, 26 × 32". Whitney Museum of American Art, New York; Purchase 36.153.
Photograph by Geoffrey Clements, © 1996 Whitney Museum of American Art.

What did you notice first when you looked at this painting? What did you notice next?

Where do you see vertical lines in the painting? Horizontal lines? Diagonal ones? How do the lines in this painting affect where your eye moves when looking at the scene?

Observe the colors in this painting. What colors do you see repeated in several places?

Do you like the scene depicted in this painting? Why or why not?

John Sloan (1871–1951) belonged to a group named "the Ashcan School" by critics because they thought their art looked like trash! Nothing could be further from the truth. Sloan and his colleagues called themselves "The Eight" because there were eight of them. They created art that explored the ordinary life of people in large cities.

At that time, the early 1900s, the cities were growing very quickly as the economy became industrialized. Sloan and his group considered large cities to be the heart and soul of America. They were constantly inspired by the daily experiences of city dwellers. But art critics did not want to see the harsh realities of life in paintings. They preferred more idealized and peaceful scenes.

Sloan painted scenes of the people he saw around him—in tenement building backyards, on dirty streets, and in grimy restaurants. *Backyards, Greenwich Village* is a typical painting. At this time, Sloan was experimenting with a limited palette of colors. He would only use about ten colors and mix them to create various shades. The palette is evident in *Backyards, Greenwich Village*. In purples, greens, and whites, the picture depicts a snowy backyard in New York City. Children build a snowman, clothes dry on a line, and an alley cat spies on the children from the top of a snow-covered shed. On the right, a little girl looks out a window at another cat. Overall, the white snow serves to brighten the entire scene.

JOSEPH STELLA. *The Brooklyn Bridge: Variation on an Old Theme.*
1939. Oil on canvas, 70 × 42". Collection of Whitney Museum of American Art, New York; Purchase 42.15.
Photograph by Sandak, Inc., © 1999 Whitney Museum of American Art.

Describe the lines and shapes you see in this painting.

Do you think this scene is during the day or at night? What makes you think so?

Does this look like a photograph of a bridge to you? How is it like or not like a photograph?

How would you feel about walking across this bridge? Explain.

Joseph Stella (1877–1946) first saw the Brooklyn Bridge when he emigrated to the United States from a small town in Italy when he was nineteen years old. He was immediately fascinated with the bridge, and perhaps even more so by New York City and its many skyscrapers. He walked around the city whenever he could, sketching scenes and buildings that aroused his interest. Life for a young immigrant could be hard, and Stella often found comfort in solitary walks across the large Brooklyn Bridge.

Stella became known as a "Futurist" painter because he depicted machinery, force, power, and contemporary structures in his paintings. Everyone considered these as crucial elements in society's progress toward an ever-more promising future. Futurists often painted objects as they might look when they were in motion. They did this by using overlapping images and repeating lines. Although he is well known for his Futurist paintings, Stella also worked in several other styles during his lifetime.

Stella used the Brooklyn Bridge in many of his pictures. In this painting, he makes the famous bridge look as if it were being seen through broken glass by depicting it with sharp, clean lines and repeating shapes. Stella presents the bridge as a viewer would see it from the pedestrian walkway, with the city looming in the distance through the two arches at the top. In a separate lower panel, the bridge and the city sit side by side, framed in rays of light.

GRANT WOOD. *Stone City, Iowa.*
1930. Oil on wood panel, 30¼ × 40″. Joslyn Museum, Omaha, Nebraska.
Art © Estate of Grant Wood / Licensed by VAGA, New York, NY.

Notice the striped pattern made by the plants in the field in the foreground. What other patterns or repeated shapes can you find in this painting?

What objects in the painting appear to be moving? Why do you think that is?

How many people can you see here? How many animals?

What does this town have in common with the place where you live? What are some differences?

Grant Wood (1891–1942) was born on a farm in Iowa near the town of Stone City, the subject of this painting. He had a strong emotional connection to his home state and spent most of his life there. As a painter, Wood is best known for his images of Iowa's small towns and farms.

Wood created his most famous paintings during the Great Depression, a period that lasted from 1929 into the late 1930s when many Americans lost their jobs and struggled with poverty. Despite the difficulties of the time, Wood's scenes, including *Stone City, Iowa*, often show peaceful, seemingly untroubled places. There are no obviously poor people in this painting, and the buildings appear to be in good repair. Wood was one of the artists known as "Regionalists," whose 1930s work was characterized by their subjects: ordinary country and small-town life in the Midwestern part of the United States.

In his painting *Stone City, Iowa*, Wood included many real details— such as the vertical boards on the barn in the foreground. But he also simplified much of the scene. The hills, for instance, appear perfectly smooth. In addition, Wood made a few changes in the landscape. He "moved" the location of some hills and made them bigger or smaller than they really were! So while this picture shows an actual place, Wood altered our view of it to make the painting's composition and design more to his and, he hoped, his viewers' liking.

WILLIAM H. JOHNSON. *Jitterbugs I.*
c. 1940–41. Oil on wood. 39¾ × 31″. Smithsonian American Art Museum, Washington, DC.
Photo credit: Smithsonian American Art Museum, Washington, DC / Art Resource, NY.

What shapes do you see in this painting? How are shapes used to form the people and the setting?

Make a list of five basic colors you think might have been on Johnson's palette. Where do you see colors repeated?

Do you think this couple is having a good time? How can you tell?

Create a story about the couple you see in this painting.

William H. Johnson (1901 – 70) taught himself to draw by copying newspaper cartoons. He moved to New York City from South Carolina at the age of seventeen. Johnson felt that as an African American he would have more freedom and opportunity there. He worked two jobs to pay his tuition at the National Academy of Design. In 1926, he moved to Paris, where he was influenced by many other artists.

With the exception of a brief return to the United States in 1930, Johnson remained in Europe until 1938. Back in New York, he joined the Federal Art Project, a program funded by the Works Progress Administration, the WPA. The WPA was a federal agency that provided jobs for the unemployed, many of them artists, during the Great Depression of the 1930s. Johnson taught painting at the Harlem Community Art Center. In his own work, he was inspired by the current exuberant artistic, musical, and cultural environment in the north Manhattan neighborhood of Harlem. The famous Savoy Ballroom, just a few steps away from the Art Center, was a prime source.

In *Jitterbugs I*, Johnson presents an African-American couple whose dancing conveys the energy and confidence coming out of Harlem at that time. The artist uses a dynamic painting style of flat-looking figures composed of geometric shapes and blocks of color. The word "jitterbug" itself refers to the ballroom dance then popular not only in Harlem but all over America. The word was also applied to slang, lifestyles, and clothing styles.

DIEGO RIVERA. *The Flower Vendor (Girl with Lilies).*
1941. Oil on Masonite, 48 × 48″. Norton Simon Museum, Pasadena, CA, Gift of Mr. Cary Grant, 1980. © 2007 Banco de México
Diego Rivera & Frida Kahlo Museums Trust. Av. Cinco de Mayo No. 2, Col. Centro, Del. Cuauhtémoc 06059, México, D.F.

What do you notice about the size of the girl in this painting compared with the size of her flowers?

How has the artist used lines and shapes to create patterns? Point out the patterns that you can find.

The title of this painting is *The Flower Vendor (Girl with Lilies)*. Where do you think this girl might be selling her flowers?

What expression do you think this girl has on her face?

Diego Rivera (1886–1957) was very proud of being a Mexican and of being a Mexican artist. During his life, however, he lived in several different countries, including Spain, France, and Italy, where he learned a variety of art techniques. Rivera combined what he learned with elements of traditional Mexican painting to create his own style. Among these elements were very simplified forms and bright, vivid colors. Rivera also often used the national colors of Mexico—red, white, and green—which are those on the Mexican flag. In addition, he frequently included common symbols of Mexico in his paintings, such as calla lilies, baskets, and hats.

Rivera was famous for his murals, or wall paintings. By painting on the walls of buildings in Mexico and the United States, Rivera was able to introduce his work into the everyday lives of many people. Because he was interested in politics and history, Rivera's murals often re-created famous scenes from Mexico's past. He also painted native Mexican people and their traditions.

Rivera certainly demonstrated his love for his native Mexico and its people in *The Flower Vendor (Girl with Lilies)*. The flowers are calla lilies, which are native to Mexico. The artist depicts them as tall, strong, and bright, using a style that incorporates aspects of traditional Mexican art. The flat shapes and bright colors are distinctly Mexican. The repetitive shapes of the flowers recall ancient Mexican paintings, which often featured patterns of varying shapes.

GEORGIA O'KEEFFE. *Autumn Leaves No. 2.*
1927. Oil on canvas, 32 × 21″. Private Collection. © 2008 Georgia O'Keeffe Museum /
Artists Rights Society (ARS), New York. Photo credit: Art Resource, NY.

What colors do you see in this painting?

How would you describe the shapes you see? Are there geometric shapes— squares, circles, and triangles? Are there free-form shapes?

Do these leaves look like ones you have seen before? How are they similar or different?

Where do you think the artist might have observed these leaves?

Georgia O'Keeffe (1887–1986) grew up on a farm in Sun Prairie, Wisconsin. She was the second of seven children, and received art lessons at home. After studying at the Art Institute of Chicago, she moved to New York, where her work gradually began to be recognized. She married the famous photographer Alfred Stieglitz, with whom she worked. Her farm childhood was a life-long influence on her artwork. O'Keeffe is known for the boldness of her nature subjects and scenes.

Throughout her career, O'Keeffe tried hard to find her own language in painting. She was not interested in painting things exactly as they looked in real life. She wanted to create art that could also express her feelings and ideas. O'Keeffe painted objects as only she saw them, not as others saw them. She painted small pieces of nature, such as flowers and leaves, on very large scale.

While living in the desert country of New Mexico, O'Keeffe created her well-known paintings of flowers, bones, stones, and skulls. However, she spent much of her early life living and painting in Lake George, New York, a semi-rural community in the Adirondack Mountains. *Autumn Leaves No. 2* was painted at Lake George. The orange, purple, brown, and yellow shades give the observer a definite feeling of autumn. The close-up view and exaggerated colors make the leaf seem abstract, thus causing the viewer to pay attention to the shapes, colors, and lines hidden within it.

LOUIS COMFORT TIFFANY. *Landscape.*
Stained glass window. Private collection. Photo credit: Art Resource, NY.

Describe the scene you see in the design of this window.

What time of day do you think is represented in the scene?
What season of the year?

Why do you think the artist included columns and steps in the design of this window?

Would you like to have a window like this in your home? Why or why not?

Louis Comfort Tiffany (1848–1933) first intended to become a painter. But after taking a glassmaking class, he realized he preferred working with glass. He began by designing stained glass windows, using the current technique in which colors were painted onto the glass. Within ten years Tiffany had invented a new method, which involved actually dyeing the glass instead of just painting on its surface. Separate glass pieces were then bound together with leading, like a puzzle, to form the final scene or design.

Tiffany also designed many affordable household objects, such as vases, bowls, jewelry, furniture, and textiles. He worked mostly during the time of the "Arts & Crafts" movement, which began in Europe in the late nineteenth century, and spread to America in the early years of the twentieth century. The movement encouraged the idea of using artistic designs for everyday objects. Artists thought less about how objects were used and more about their shape and overall look. Nature themes were also important to Arts & Crafts designers. Many of Tiffany's creations depicted flowers, plants, landscapes, and other natural forms.

Tiffany created his compositions very carefully. The window design pictured here is symmetrical, with columns on each side and the river dividing the scene down the center. Although the window is flat and two-dimensional, Tiffany composed the scene in such a way that the viewer feels as if he or she could walk right out of the window and into the beautiful day.

ANDY WARHOL. *Muhammad Ali.*
1977. Synthetic polymer paint and silkscreen ink on canvas, 40″ × 40″. © 2008 Andy Warhol Foundation
for the Visual Arts / ARS, NY. Photo credit: Andy Warhol Foundation, Inc. / Art Resource, NY.

How is this print similar to a photograph? How is it different?

What do you notice about the way colors appear on this print?

How do you think the artist felt about Muhammad Ali? What evidence can you find in the artwork to support your opinion?

Would you want to hang this work in your home? Why or why not?

American artist Andrew Warhola (1928–87) began his career doing commercial illustration and designing store-window displays. When his first illustrations appeared in a magazine, his name was mistakenly printed as Andy Warhol. The new name stuck!

Because of his early experience with advertising, Warhol was very knowledgeable about how to please his audience. His art used many images from popular culture, such as the Campbell's soup can and the dollar sign. Warhol was intrigued by celebrities, and as a result he created large prints of many famous people. The process he used to create his prints allowed him to make many versions of one picture—the same, yet with slight variations in each one.

In addition to being an artist, Andy Warhol became a self-made media star. He owned a loft in New York City he called the Factory, where he threw huge parties that were attended by famous artists and actors. Warhol felt it was very important for him to become famous, but at the same time he criticized how easy it was to do so.

Warhol made several images of Muhammad Ali, a worldwide boxing sensation in the 1960s and 1970s. Ali captured people's imagination and attention with his unique boxing style, ability to compose rhymes, and many self-promotions. "I am the greatest!" Ali was known to declare. In this print, Warhol depicts the power of Muhammad Ali's fists and personality by using dramatic colors and jagged lines.

HELEN FRANKENTHALER. *Blue Territory.*
1955. Oil on canvas, 113 × 58″. Whitney Museum of American Art, New York; Purchase, with funds from the Whitney Museum of American Art, 57.8. Photograph by Sandak, Inc., © 2002 Whitney Museum of American Art.

What colors do you see in this painting?

What does this painting make you think about? How does it make you feel?

Why do you think Frankenthaler titled this painting *Blue Territory*? What title would you give this painting?

Helen Frankenthaler (born 1928) deliberately leaves sections of her canvas blank so they can "breathe." To her, canvas isn't merely the material used to hold paint. Rather, the texture, the color, and other traits of the canvas are important elements in the creation of her paintings.

Frankenthaler invented a style of painting called "Color Field Art," which involves soaking canvases with layers, or "fields," of color. She sets her huge canvases on the floor and, instead of applying paint with a brush, she pours paint on top of it. With this technique, the final design of the work is determined both by the artist and by how the paint happens to flow, overlap, and react with air and gravity. Frankenthaler's paintings do not contain recognizable objects; instead, they glow with color and movement. This is because the artist does not try to paint things as they exist in real life. She paints "abstracted" works, which means that she reduces objects to their basic line, shape, color, and texture.

Frankenthaler's artwork is based in nature—both real and imagined. Many people say that her paintings, like *Blue Territory*, resemble abstracted scenes from nature. The flowing shapes and movement in her work are reminiscent of water and wind. Frankenthaler is best known for the intense color of her paintings and the feelings they evoke in viewers.

---------------- ✦ ----------------

Go back and look through the pages of this book again.

Which artwork is your favorite for today? Why?

Which artist interests you the most? Why?

Do any of the artworks confuse you? How so?

Which artwork reminds you of something in your own life?

Return to the art in this book another time. You may notice new things and have new ideas each time you look.

Keep looking!
